my Creative writing journal

unique prompts, exercises, and activities to inspire your imagination

KRISTINE PIDKAMENY

CICO BOOKS
LONDON NEW YORK

Published in 2021 by CICO Books
An imprint of Ryland Peters & Small Ltd
20–21 Jockey's Fields   341 E 116th St
London WC1R 4BW   New York, NY 10029

www.rylandpeters.com

10 9 8 7 6 5 4 3 2 1

A CIP catalog record for this book is available from the Library of
Congress and the British Library.

ISBN: 978-1-78249-924-4

Printed in China

Senior editor: Carmel Edmonds
Senior designer: Emily Breen
Art director: Sally Powell
Head of production: Patricia Harrington
Publishing manager: Penny Craig
Publisher: Cindy Richards

Contents

Introduction

We are always creating whether we realize it or not. Often what we create happens out of seemingly nothing. An idea suddenly arises during your daily routine, perhaps while staring out a window, taking a walk, or brushing your teeth. You wonder, "Now, where did that come from?" In the details of our daily experience there's an endless flow of ideas just waiting for us to tap into. Conversations, movements, memories, ways of dressing, having a meal—the inspiration for our creative writing is endless. Through noticing contrast we can recognize how every day is truly transformative. We change through the hours from morning to evening. Pay attention. Reflect on your experiences and observations. Jot down that idea. Express that feeling in words. You can always come back later to expand upon these things. Remain curious and appreciate the creative surprises.

A look inside

A number-one benefit of writing in a journal is that it allows you the space to find your voice. Through expanding your knowledge, experience, and self-expression, you will discover new insight into your writing process. Designed to nurture your creativity and self-motivation, this journal provides welcome guidance, inspiration, and plenty of writing room. With unique prompts, topics, and inspiring mantras, a variety of suggestions are offered to spark your imagination. The eight journal sections are set up for ease and flexibility. You can follow the sections in the order they are organized from start to finish—or, if you prefer, dip in and out of the different sections, depending on how you're feeling or what goals you have in mind at the time of your writing session. The writing exercises will have you brainstorming new ideas and help you start to write longer pieces—perhaps even leading to your first novel, short story, or memoir.

Writing tips and helpful habits

Writing is a solitary yet rich experience. Whether you're new to journal writing or find yourself really stuck in the creative process, the motivation to get started and the encouragement to continue are key. Being aware of helpful habits and feeling supported goes a long way.

• Do set aside a time for journal writing in your day, every day. It is the most important commitment to keep, so make it one you look forward to. Figure out a realistic time in your daily schedule. Decide upon the length of time you will write.

Choose a favorable and comfortable location. And show up, even on those days you'd rather not. The muse is waiting, always—no matter how you are feeling.

• Create a ritual before you begin and close your writing sessions. This can be grounding and reinforces showing up to write every day. Before you begin, you create a cue for your brain to switch to writing mode. In closing, you acknowledge the end of your session. Maybe you play a favorite piece of music, prepare a particular beverage, position your writing materials, meditate, or light a candle. Do whatever works best for you and choose something you personally enjoy.

• Remember to recharge and pace yourself. It is important to take breaks during your writing sessions. This keeps your energy balanced, focused, and productive. Get up and walk around, stretch, shake your body and hands a bit, and have a glass of water to stay hydrated.

• Choose a writing touchstone or talisman, a meaningful token to keep you company while you are writing. It could be a stone, photograph, quote or mantra, piece of jewelry, coin, or favorite pen, or maybe even a collection of a few of these items kept nearby while you write. It can be helpful to be in the company of friendly reminders.

• Accept the times you might question your writing ability and whether you are good enough. It is a natural part of the creative process. Welcome the opportunity to deepen the conversation with yourself—it will free you up. Allow the unsettling feeling and then imagine yourself moving forward. Visualize yourself continuing to write despite fear of failure—and then you will.

• It's a good idea, as well as journaling, to read how other writers write and be inspired by their work. Return to your favorite books and think beyond the story and characters. Consider the author's writing style and expression.

In the course of our lives, each day we build upon the one before. The same holds true with our creativity and writing. Inside this interactive journal, you will be able to get your thoughts, feelings, and words on paper. You will become a better writer, enjoy your writing journey, and even learn more about yourself.

Believe in your ideas

Be supported and reminded of why you want to write in the first place. Once a week for one month, send yourself a postcard or electronic message of encouragement and appreciation for your creativity, focus, and unique voice as a writer. Keep track of your progress here. Include the date sent and a brief uplifting mantra you create from the words in your message.

Where to Begin

Quick warm-up prompts

to get started

List six things that immediately make you feel happy.

1

2

3

4

5

6

What is your favorite room at home and what do you like to do there?

List six things you are looking forward to.

1

2

3

4

5

6

List six things you are relieved to leave behind.

1

2

3

4

5

6

Look up from where you are now and describe what you see.

Look down from where you are now and describe what you see.

Choose an object in your surroundings to focus on.
Close your eyes and imagine this object in great detail.
Open your eyes and write out the details.

What season of the year do you enjoy the most and why?

How do you celebrate your birthday?

What makes you smile?

_____
_____
_____
_____
_____
_____
_____
_____
_____
_____
_____
_____
_____

What makes you feel sad?

_____
_____
_____
_____
_____
_____
_____
_____
_____
_____
_____
_____
_____
_____

What are five qualities you appreciate about yourself?

1

2

3

4

5

Describe something beautiful you saw today.

Open your eyes and see the beauty that surrounds you

Note any writing inspirations here.

_____
_____
_____
_____
_____
_____
_____
_____
_____
_____
_____
_____
_____
_____

Name five places in the world you've always wanted to visit and why.

1

2

3

4

5

Name five different uses for a suitcase aside from a piece of luggage for a trip.

1

2

3

4

5

Imagine one thing you'd rather be doing now than writing in this journal.

Which authors are on your top ten list and why?

1

2

3

4

5

6

7

8

9

10

What is your favorite movie or TV series and why?

Which animated character do you most identify with and why?

Ask yourself: WHY do you want to write?

Ask yourself: HOW is writing important in your life?

Word Play

Fun exercises to expand your

appreciation of words

Choose three of your favorite words and use each one in a sentence.

1

2

3

Choose three words that you dislike and use each one in a sentence.

1

2

3

Create a list of associations for the following words:

travel

weather

food

sleep

clothes

home

fun

love

friends

work

family

beginnings

endings

time

color

truth

Set a timer for five minutes and list all the verbs that immediately come to mind.

Set a timer for five minutes and list all the adjectives that immediately come to mind.

Set a timer for five minutes and list all the nouns that immediately come to mind.

Set a timer for five minutes and list all the adverbs that immediately come to mind.

Cut out inspiring words and phrases from magazines and newspapers
to create a collage that makes you feel energized.

Amaze yourself today

Open the dictionary and randomly choose five words, then write a separate
sentence for each word.

1

2

3

4

5

What is a favorite phrase or reply you frequently use in conversation or writing?

Create three new ways to reword the above phrase or reply.

1

2

3

Pick five adjectives that describe your favorite piece of clothing.
Write five sentences, one for each adjective, on a different topic.

Adjective 1:

Sentence:

Adjective 2:

Sentence:

Adjective 3:

Sentence:

Adjective 4:

Sentence:

Adjective 5:

Sentence:

Scan an article or random page of a book and write down all the words that immediately appeal to you. Create a micro story with these words.

Remember

Mining the past and the riches

of self-reflection

Recall a favorite scent from childhood and the feeling it evokes.

_____
_____
_____
_____
_____
_____
_____
_____
_____
_____
_____
_____

Write about your earliest memory in life.

_____
_____
_____
_____
_____
_____
_____
_____
_____
_____
_____
_____
_____
_____

Name two close friends from your teenage years and how you met.
Are you still in contact with each other?

1
_____
_____
_____
_____
_____

2
_____
_____
_____
_____
_____

Who was your first best friend in life?

_____
_____
_____
_____
_____
_____
_____
_____
_____
_____
_____
_____
_____
_____

Look back on your best summer vacation.

Call to mind the details of a delicious meal and describe what made it so enjoyable. Was it the food, the preparation, the company, the place where it was eaten— or perhaps you were just very hungry at the time?

Describe your childhood kitchen.

What beliefs or assumptions from your past have held you back?

Recall a challenging situation that made you more resilient.

Broken crayons still color

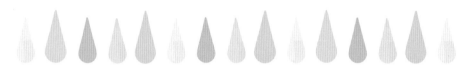

Note any writing inspirations here.

_____
_____
_____
_____
_____
_____
_____
_____
_____
_____
_____
_____
_____
_____
_____
_____
_____
_____
_____
_____
_____
_____

Describe a pleasant experience from your past.

_____

_____

_____

_____

_____

_____

_____

_____

_____

_____

_____

_____

_____

Describe an unpleasant experience from your past.

_____

_____

_____

_____

_____

_____

_____

_____

_____

_____

_____

_____

What was your favorite book, story, or folk tale from childhood?

What was your top choice activity growing up? Does it still have a place in your life now?

Write about a recent night dream or daydream.

Re-read what you wrote above and note any new insights or symbols
that come to mind.

Think back to yesterday and detail your day from start to finish.

What was the highlight of your day?

Listen with your heart and answer the call

Note any writing inspirations here.

_____

_____

_____

_____

_____

_____

_____

_____

_____

_____

_____

_____

_____

_____

Write about one of your biggest goals or ambitions.

Describe a do-over for a past experience.

Think about a teacher, mentor, or boss who inspired you
and how they changed your life.

What was your favorite subject in school and why?

Recall the first movie you ever saw.
Where were you and who were you with?

_____

_____

_____

_____

_____

_____

_____

_____

_____

_____

Remember the first time you did something on your own.

_____

_____

_____

_____

_____

_____

_____

_____

_____

_____

_____

Write a letter to someone you've lost touch with.

Write a letter to someone you'd like to forgive.

Describe a moment of uncontrollable laughter or time of happy celebration.

Recall the first time you felt really scared or nervous.

Make a list of big surprises in your life so far.

Choose one surprise from the list above and describe it in detail.

What If...?

Creative play to spark

your imagination

If you were a pair of shoes, what kind would you be?
Where would you have been and where would you be going?

If you were a cocktail or mocktail, what name would you go by?
List your ingredients and describe your usual consumer.

If you were a tree, what kind would you be and where would you be planted?

If you were a building, how many windows would you have and what would you look upon?

If you could be teleported anywhere in the world, where would you go and what would you do there?

If you became a millionaire tomorrow, what life changes would you make and why?

If you were a suitcase, what would you look like and what would you contain? Where would you be traveling, and who would be taking you there?

If you were an important figure in history, who would you be and why?

If you were an invisible person, where would you frequent? Who would you prefer to observe, and what would their conversations be about?

If you were a dance, what particular style would you be? Who would do your dance, and where would they do it?

Find your dance

Note any writing inspirations here.

_____

_____

_____

_____

_____

_____

_____

_____

_____

_____

_____

_____

_____

_____

_____

_____

_____

_____

_____

_____

If you were a day of the week, which one would you be and why?

If you were a piece of furniture, what would you be, what would you be made of, and which room would you be located in?

If you were a devious character in a novel, who would you be and what would motivate your actions?

If you were an honorable character in a novel, who would you be and what would you value most in life?

If you were an animal living in the wild, where would you live and what would be your favorite activities?

If you were a domesticated animal, what would your home life be like?

If you were a color of the rainbow, which one would you be and why?

If you were a season, which one would you be?
Describe the people that would enjoy you and how you would benefit them.

If you were a sweater, what kind would you be? Where and when would people wear you?

_____

_____

_____

_____

_____

_____

_____

_____

_____

_____

_____

_____

If you were a piece of jewelry, what would you be and what would you be made of?

_____

_____

_____

_____

_____

_____

_____

_____

_____

If you were a plant, what kind would you be? How big would you be and where would you live?

If you were a flower, what kind would you be? Describe your fragrance and color. Would you mark any special events?

Live, laugh, love

Note any writing inspirations here.

_____

_____

_____

_____

_____

_____

_____

_____

_____

_____

_____

_____

_____

_____

_____

_____

_____

_____

_____

_____

_____

If you were a greeting card, what occasion would you be celebrating?
Compose your message to the receiver.

_____

_____

_____

_____

_____

_____

_____

_____

_____

_____

_____

If you were a ride in an amusement park, which one would you be and who
would you take for a ride?

_____

_____

_____

_____

_____

_____

_____

_____

_____

_____

_____

_____

If you were a beverage, what kind would you be and what would be your brand name? Describe your usual consumer.

_____

_____

_____

_____

_____

_____

_____

_____

_____

_____

If you were a dessert, what would you taste like? List your ingredients. Where would you be served?

_____

_____

_____

_____

_____

_____

_____

_____

_____

_____

_____

If you were an item in a classified ad, what would you be?
Describe your key selling points.

If you were a mode of transportation, what kind would you be?
Where would you travel to, and how would you benefit your passengers?

If you were a form of exercise, what would you be?
Who would be your biggest fans and why?

If you were a scientist, what kind would you be?
What would be your biggest discovery that helped the world?

If you were born in a different era, which time period would you live in?
How would your life be different from now?

If you were a superhero, what would be your name?
What would be your superpowers?

Sensing

Exploring sensory experiences

to broaden awareness

Welcome the quiet and focus on the sound and sensation of slowly inhaling and exhaling five times. Describe the details of the experience.

Write about how you felt before and after. Did you notice any difference?

Looking out of a window, describe the shapes and colors you see.

Explain the sky to a person without sight.

Take a walk outdoors after it rains or snows. Listen to your feet touching the ground. Describe the sound and rhythm your feet make and how it feels moving them between steps.

What does rain or snow smell like?

Open the refrigerator when you are really hungry.
Describe your total sensory experience.

Listen to the sounds around you. How many do you hear and what are they?

Pay attention to your breath while walking outdoors. Can you hear it and does it have a texture you can name? Do you notice any difference in the rhythm and quality of your breath the longer you focus on it?

Sit in a public place where various people are talking. Listen to the conversations as if the sounds the words make create a piece of music. What is the theme and what would you title this piece?

Remember to listen

Note any writing inspirations here.

_____
_____
_____
_____
_____
_____
_____
_____
_____
_____
_____
_____
_____
_____
_____
_____
_____
_____

Explain the sound of a clock ticking to a person who cannot hear.

Describe an orange to a person without sight or a sense of smell or taste.

What does a warm seaside breeze feel like as it blows across your face and through your hair?

What does a sudden gust of wind on a cold city day feel like?

Choose your most comfortable item of clothing.
Describe how it affects your senses.

_____

_____

_____

_____

_____

_____

_____

_____

_____

_____

_____

Describe an article of clothing you find most uncomfortable,
though need to wear at times.

_____

_____

_____

_____

_____

_____

_____

_____

_____

_____

_____

_____

_____

Which aromas do you find most relaxing and why?

Which aromas do you find most pungent and why?

Using sensory words to describe experiences adds dimension and makes writing more memorable. Create a list of power words associated with the following words:

sight

smell

touch

taste

hearing

motion

Describe a particular experience using some of the words from your lists on the opposite page.

Point of View

Closer observations and ways to

switch perspective

Choose a famous person you admire and write from their perspective what a typical day is like for them.

Pick a headline from a news story that appeals to you.
Do not read the article. Instead, write your own.

Imagine you are paying for your groceries at the supermarket. Based on your purchases and behavior during the transaction, how would the cashier describe you to their co-workers?

A dog sits alone in a parked car on a busy street.
What do they see, why are they there, and who are they waiting for?

You notice a cat sleeping in the window of a storefront.
Picture a typical day for them.

Stand up from where you are sitting and walk around a bit—through a doorway if possible. Sit down in a different location. Write about your observations.

Be brave enough to take a step into a different world

Note any writing inspirations here.

_____

_____

_____

_____

_____

_____

_____

_____

_____

_____

_____

_____

_____

_____

Imagine you have switched lives with your one of your neighbors.
How would they describe your daily routine?

Walking on a crowded street, you unexpectedly run into someone you haven't
seen in years. How would they recount your meeting?

Connect more closely to the world around you today, whether indoors or outdoors. Keep track of any signs or symbols you feel strongly attracted to. Repeat for a few days. Did you notice any coincidences?

Reach for what you think is unreachable

Note any writing inspirations here.

_____
_____
_____
_____
_____
_____
_____
_____
_____
_____
_____
_____
_____
_____
_____
_____
_____

Travel an unfamiliar path to one of your usual destinations. What did you notice?

At home, work, or school, or on your commute, choose a different seat from where you typically sit. Describe what is new in your experience.

Choose a photograph or artwork and describe what you see
and how it makes you feel.

_____
_____
_____
_____
_____
_____
_____
_____
_____
_____
_____

With the same photograph or artwork, now imagine yourself a part of it.
Which part are you? Describe how it feels looking out at the viewer.

_____
_____
_____
_____
_____
_____
_____
_____
_____
_____
_____
_____
_____

Empty your shoulder bag, knapsack, or purse. Randomly choose four items and describe why they are important to have with you. Any unexpected discoveries?

While traveling, you are stuck in traffic or your plane or train is delayed. What are your fellow travelers or passengers thinking about?

Wake up a little before sunrise. Sit in early morning darkness and observe the changes in your environment and within yourself as daylight fills the room.

A little before sunset, sit in a room with only natural lighting. Observe the changes around you and within you as the room shifts to natural darkness.

Sit on a chair, sofa, or bed and describe what you see in the room at eye level.

_____

_____

_____

_____

_____

_____

_____

_____

_____

_____

_____

Lie down on the floor in the same room, now looking up at the ceiling.
Describe the room from this vantage point and what it feels like.

_____

_____

_____

_____

_____

_____

_____

_____

_____

_____

_____

You are online or on the phone with a customer service agent concerning a recent problem with one of your bills. If you were the agent, how would you respond to the situation?

_____

_____

_____

_____

_____

_____

_____

_____

_____

_____

Write a dialog between you and an alien who has just landed on earth.

_____

_____

_____

_____

_____

_____

_____

_____

_____

_____

_____

_____

_____

Look up from this journal. Write about what you see in front of you and what you imagine is behind you.

Take a walk outdoors and imagine all that is going on beneath your feet.

Adventure is waiting for you

Note any writing inspirations here.

_____
_____
_____
_____
_____
_____
_____
_____
_____
_____
_____
_____
_____
_____
_____
_____
_____
_____
_____

Describe the difference between talking face to face with a person or having a conversation through an electronic device.

_____
_____
_____
_____
_____
_____
_____
_____
_____
_____
_____
_____
_____

Choose a favorite photograph, image, or artwork and turn it upside down. Describe what you see and how it makes you feel.

_____
_____
_____
_____
_____
_____
_____
_____
_____
_____
_____
_____

In a class you used to attend (or still attend) regularly as a student, imagine you are now the teacher. Describe the experience and how the class would be different.

_____
_____
_____
_____
_____
_____
_____
_____
_____
_____
_____

You are in a disagreement with a family member, close friend, or colleague regarding an important issue that is meaningful to both of you. Describe the experience from the other person's viewpoint.

_____
_____
_____
_____
_____
_____
_____
_____
_____
_____

In a public setting you are delighted to see your favorite author, so you introduce yourself to them. What's their first impression of you?

A friend is also with you. What's their impression of the interaction between you and the author?

While traveling throughout your day, take special notice of your surroundings. Keep a list of what stands out to you—perhaps an unusual passer-by, an enticing aroma, a curious sound, nature, an event taking place, or the details of the sidewalk or road.

Compose a short paragraph or poem based on your above list.

Objects, Places, Experiences

Finding inspiration everywhere

around you

Choose four items from your junk drawer. Give a short history on each one.
What do these items reveal about your lifestyle?

1

2

3

4

A genie has granted you three wishes. What are they?

1

2

3

It's still free to dream

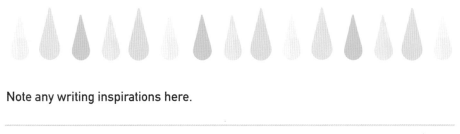

Note any writing inspirations here.

You've discovered a secret passageway in your neighborhood. Where does it lead to, what goes on in this place, and who will you find there? Will you tell others about your discovery?

What is the one physical item you cherish most in your life now and why?

How would your life unfold if you lost this item forever?
What would happen if you eventually found this item 20 years later?

Disengage from "what's next" thinking mode for five minutes and allow yourself to be bored. Describe how you felt both before and after the experience.

Continue to do the previous exercise every day for one week. At the end of the week, note any changes in your attention and sense of time.

What is your favorite type of hat or headgear? Is it for function or style, or maybe both? What does it say about your personality and lifestyle?

Open your dresser sock drawer and pick out a pair at random.
Describe this pair of socks in detail and where they have traveled recently.

Describe the patterns on the side of a building, a room's flooring, or in the grain of wood on a table. Where do they lead you?

_____

_____

_____

_____

_____

_____

_____

_____

_____

_____

_____

Do you prefer outdoor or indoor activities and why?

_____

_____

_____

_____

_____

_____

_____

_____

_____

_____

_____

_____

You've been nominated as the author of the best banned book of the year award. What is the title of your book and what is it about?

You have lost this journal. What reward would you offer to the person who finds it?

The billboard you created is put up on a frequently traveled roadway. What does it say, who is it meant for, and where is it located?

You are the centerpiece item in a shop window display. Describe what kind of shop this is and what you see around you.

How does your current home or neighborhood environment affect you?

How does your current work or school environment affect you?

What book or books are on your nightstand now?

Imagine you are seated next to your favorite author on a long airplane flight.
The conversation is flowing. What are you talking about?

Trust your instinct

Note any writing inspirations here.

_____

_____

_____

_____

_____

_____

_____

_____

_____

_____

_____

_____

_____

_____

_____

_____

_____

_____

_____

Close your eyes. Write about the first thought that comes to mind.

Taking It Further

Longer writing exercises to keep

your creativity flowing

Free writing exercise: set a timer for 15 minutes and let your thoughts run loosely on the page.

Re-read quickly what you wrote on the previous page and highlight the words that immediately and intuitively pop off the page to you. Take these words and connect them into an idea or story.

With your nondominant hand, write two sentences describing yourself. Repeat the exercise every day for a week.

Monday

Tuesday

Wednesday

Thursday

Friday

Saturday

Sunday

Describe your experience of the previous exercise. Were you aware of a change in your thought process, or a different way of seeing yourself and your sense of time, as you progressed through the week?

Dedicate one week to add one new word a day to your vocabulary. Use each word in a sentence.

Monday

Tuesday

Wednesday

Thursday

Friday

Saturday

Sunday

At the end of the week, incorporate all seven new words from the previous page into a short story.

On a familiar route you walk every day, notice three new things you see.
Repeat every day for a week and keep a list here.

Monday
1
2
3

Tuesday
1
2
3

Wednesday
1
2
3

Thursday
1
2
3

Friday
1
2
3

Saturday
1
2
3

Sunday
1
2
3

After completing the previous exercise, compose a micro story
or poem based on your list.

Show up and embrace possibility

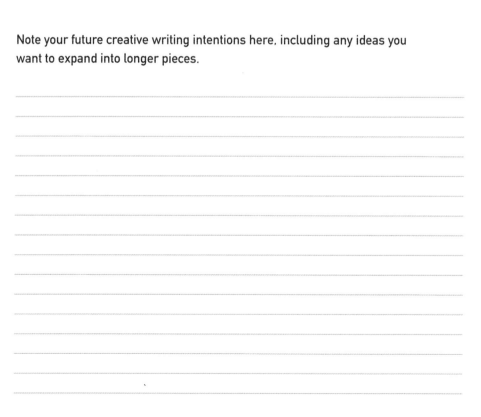

Note your future creative writing intentions here, including any ideas you want to expand into longer pieces.